First Repertoire for
CELLO

with piano

Book One

Selected, edited and
arranged by

**Pat Legg
and
Alan Gout**

FABER *ff* MUSIC

Contents

© 1996 by Faber Music Ltd
First published in 1996 by Faber Music Ltd
3 Queen Square London WC1N 3AU
Cover illustration by John Levers
Cover design by S & M Tucker
Music processed by Wessex Music Services
Printed in England
All rights reserved

ISBN 0-571-51641-6

To buy Faber Music publications or to find out about the full range of titles available
please contact your local music retailer or Faber Music sales enquiries:

Faber Music Limited, Burnt Mill, Elizabeth Way, Harlow, CM20 2HX England
Tel: +44 (0)1279 82 89 82
Fax: +44 (0)1279 82 89 83
Email: sales@fabermusic.com
www.fabermusic.com

Even Steven

Howard Blake
(1938 -   )

Branle

Thoinot Arbeau
(1520 - 1595)

The Cowboy's Lament

Die Klage des Cowboys   La plainte du cowboy

American traditional
arr. A.G.

Daisy Bell

Harry Dacre
(1860 - 1922)

Away in a Manger

Krippenlied   Dans une étable

Norwegian traditional
arr. A.G.

Sonata No. 2 (4th movement)

Sonate Nr. 2 (4 Satz)   Sonate no. 2 (4e mouvement)

Stephen Paxton
(1735-1787)

Tumbalaika

Jewish traditional
arr. A.G.

The Ship's Carpenter

Der Schiffszimmermann   Le charpentier du bateau

Canadian traditional
arr. A.G.

Roly Poly

Howard Blake
(1938 -   )

Hungarian Folksong

Ungarisches Volkslied   Chant populaire hongrois

Traditional
arr. A.G.

Archangel's Lullaby

Wiegenlied des Erzengels   La berceuse de l'archange

Howard Blake
(1938 -   )

Allegretto Grazioso

John Stanley
(1712-1786)

Barcarolle

Alan Gout
(1945 -   )

Scarborough Fair

Jahrmarkt in Scarborough   La fête foraine de Scarborough

English traditional
arr. A.G.

The Fishermen's Song

Das Lied der Fischer   Le chant des pêcheurs

Highland vocal air
arr. A.G.